IDENTITIES

IDENTITIES

poems by W. R. MOSES

WESLEYAN UNIVERSITY PRESS, *Middletown, Connecticut*

Many of these poems have previously appeared elsewhere. For their cooperation, grateful acknowledgment is made to the editors of the following: *American Weave; Antioch Review; Approach; Beloit Poetry Journal; Georgia Review; Kenyon Review; Minnesota Review; The Nation; New Orleans Poetry Journal; New Republic; Northwest Review; Prairie Schooner; Sewanee Review; Whetstone; Yale Review;* and New Directions, publisher of the volume *Five Young American Poets,* 1940.

The poems named below are reprinted by authority of the journals mentioned: "Lilies" from *Massachusetts Review;* "Boy at Target Practice: A Contemplation," "Suburban Flower Store, Washington, D.C.," and "Sitting in the Woods: A Contemplation" from *The New Yorker;* "Battle Report," "Big Dam," "Contemporary Romantic," "Grackle Days," "Loon-Link," "Mummies from Alaska," "Point of View," "Sentimental Reflection," "A Trip in a Boat," "Wilson's Terns," and "Wrecked Automobiles" from *Poetry.*

Library on Congress Catalog Card Number : 65–14051
Manufactured in the United States of America
FIRST EDITION

To
E. and E.,
with love.

Contents

I

Boy at Target Practice: A Contemplation

I

Each time, greenbones, you pressed the neat trigger
You punched a new horizontal into the air.
In all of ever, those lines had not been there.

In the tumbling can those sudden, dark-rimmed holes
With revengefully sharp edges were new bits
Of subtraction. Never had other bullet hits

Made them. And when, glancing from jarred stone,
A pellet went all waspy into the sky,
That was a new parabola, a new cry.

II

Now getting caught, I think, in a sudden seeing
That everything's unique in the world's swarm
Of things, is like getting caught with nothing warm

Around you, outside when summer clouds are hailing.
It feels uncomfortable; useless, too.
We need to make ourselves (and usually do)

Protective outer garments of fat and fuzzy
Generalization; that's the way to obscure
From the ends of our nerves those sharp peltings of pure

Facts, real facts. Of course, we can't destroy them.
Not you, nor I, nor the wisest man of us
Can live with them. But aren't they marvelous?

Wilson's Terns

Rounded though slim. No angularity
Flies with the Wilson's terns that skim in lines
Of comfort, calling with sufficient grief
To make men dimly grateful there are skins
Of white soft-rounded, touchable in sorrow.
And the flittering white on the breaking blue where go
The terns over crumbling waves with fringed crests:
By common concession, a contrast soft, also.

You on the asphalt, waiting for a trolley
To clang you down to the bank, how do you know
The invisible trolley will come, the invisible bank
Show its old ugliness, seen so often by you?
You're a two-legged spider. The stood-on stone's the fact;
You make it center your web, whence mental threads
Go fasten to things you choose to exist on earth:
To women, and taxis, and wrinkle-sheeted beds.

Pike-tooth-gashed through tiny scales, and flipped
Dead on the water, a bait-minnow's factual here,
And mist is in front of the beach line. Who animalizes
With a sun-burned face and a fishpole, can he spare
Thread of the mind to tie himself to the shore?
When a tern slips out of the mist, exclaiming "Scree!"
And flaps on the minnow, and dangles it whence he came,
One need not think to the sand he cannot see.

A Trip in a Boat

The racketing boat was all that moved much
In pre-dawn darkness under the stream's mist
That sheared and shifted, eddying, cold,
Moved and went nowhere and was always there:
A good enough home for the aimless classic dead,
Or Dante's, those that groan where the gales list.

Daylight came filtering; boat's course faltered; a slough
Narrowed beside, with a shore where the weeds' way
Was poor life's also; slime-stemmed, dank,
Brown-green, brown-red, and matted and thick and fallen,
Almost unreal; but all that there was was they.

Till the birds specked out of the sky. Where sight stopped
Appearing, they largened, largened through pearl air;
Vague wings grew manifest sickle, sharp;
Small heads were certainly seen, and the trailed feet
Certainly seen. What's quite worth cherishing out,
All difficult, rare, and enlivening certainty,
Went by, in a webfoot, feathery paradigm,
Those almost tactile moments when they were there.

Contemporary Romantic

Man may be cold, alone, and melancholy;
The rain of an empty place may fall on his heart.
Wanderer on purpose, for the crosswise pleasure of it,
He may walk on the bleakest shore, all day apart.
He knows what to do with mottled sandpipers flying
Through the cold, grey air and the cold, impersonal rain.
Like the tide that threshes and weaves through the mussel rocks,
They have a catalogue number filed in his brain.

The day I saw, by the drowning end of the jetty,
A big grey fin for a moment out of the sea,
I was startled. Consulting the catalogue of romantic
Fittings, I could not place it with certainty.
It was truly unknown, and, easy in ocean violence,
Suggested the vicious strength to compel true death.
I watched it hard till it sank in the roughening water,
And remember it well, though a long time has passed.

Point of View

I wonder that a large brown owl should mouse
So near to this new loud apartment house,
Where the sweet sharp wonderful wilderness is gone
Though one thin gulley of southern trees stands on.

Why? Though paths are made, and walked to mud,
And the bloodroot all pulled out of the underwood,
And the poison ivy warred on, and left for dead,
One tree head must resemble another head

— No shoes up there — though one of them wags his beard
And the other to shapeless mould has disappeared.
There thunders the owl his eight loud hoots in the night,
And dodges eternal limbs in masterly flight

With eyes as sharp as the eyes of the herring gull
High curving over the smother that launches pull,
That will drop three hundred feet for a piece of bread
And is never fooled by a ball of paper instead.

On the Way

Though regret of process is perhaps frivolous,
It tastes like regret.

At the edge of a mud-fill
Where subsoil lies deep from the newly dug basement,
You see and sit on a pile of tree pieces
Thrown there out of the way of walls.
Looking at beech limbs and trunks of black cherry,
You think: Their rotting may warm the moon slightly,
But to hurry the change in a rapider burning
(Flushing, from a fireplace, amiable drinkers)
Would be better appreciated.

And the same in your kitchen
Sawing a board from an apple box,
When you get, astringent in your nostrils, the odor
Of fir wood, released from the dropping dust,
And think: A sorry pause on the way
For something intimate with wings lately
And light, maybe the handsomest tree
On the western ridges.

The hawk, the gliding redtail, nearly pauses
Above, reversing aim in a narrow arc.
Like points of the compass, ninety degrees of them,
His wing feathers ray, or the points of a frond of palm.

The way the eye attaches his barred bi-color
And commits his pinions, point by sun-touched point,
Whatever the wag of the world, or the day's events,
Is good, a ceremony of innocence.

Early Snow

Behindhand with its annual tax
Of leaves to operate the soil
This casual elm: still green, still green
In cloak of hope and innocence.

Now sheriff-wise, the raw November
Has gestured to enforce the law.
On leaves, and on the ground beyond,
All that deathlike white is snow.

White on the green, death on the green;
For one stare of the widening eye
The life-spin checks and then reverses:
Adonis dies as soon as born.

Expel the breath; the moment goes.
Death will not drop upon true summer.
The leaves are paid; the careless tree
Suffers no break in dendral calm,
No guilt, no incongruity.

A Fable of Bees

In remote fields, bees on the quiet flowers
Are private, and as they fly through remote air
No one notices. Back in the wood towers
An oak. Rough and unapproachable there,

Centuries safe from lightning, safe from axe,
But secretly hollow high toward its crown,
It takes the returning gatherers. They relax
Safely into that dark when night draws down,

Or rain; or stripping winter has made free
All stems of leaves, and made the fields still.
Only I know they are in the tree.
No one has tasted their honey, or ever will.

Two Attributes of Birches

Although all August I spent loving lakes,
And grew in wordless joy of all that made
Their lakehood, now that I am keen to do,
Through love, some wordy honor for their sakes,
I see most sweetly of the whole parade
The white birches by which shores are stayed,
And of all things that make their birchhood, two.

It is as though, when looking toward the shore
From the casual, quiet boat in which you ride,
You drift upon a rich green light that flows
Out of an open shell, and from the store
Of greenness that is gathered in the wide
Valves, reflects greenness. The upper side
Of the shell is growing birches; and of those

The reflection is the lower. When you put
Away that construct, beach the boat, and turn
Into the clustered brush, you presently see
An intricate bird's nest in some alder shoot;
And see the mother-builder's shrewd concern
Employed not only scraps of twig and fern,
But loose white shreds from the nearest birch tree.

The Impulse of October

October nights, wild geese string
Yelping garlands along the sky.
Mornings of light frost, grackles stutter
Beadwork jet against the sun.

Life underlines its livingness
Because below the birds, the leaf
Tacks to the inch where it shall lie
All a leaf-forever long.

He moves too, the dull wasp
Cold-diminished, for he wants,
Too, Elysian no-winter.
Stiffly angled, on basement walls

He creeps, in dusty sanctuary,
Grey substitute for the orange South.
In feeble light he is feebly seen.
The careless hand he sickly stings.

Battle Report

In the general American war between earth and pavement
I report the cruel attrition in one small pocket
Where a road-wide column of asphalt sent on patrol
Across a field has been, by a zigzag of policy,
Declared expendible. New-planted metal posts
Cut it off. No longer is any supply possible.

Its mode of fight, of course, is to hug flat
Over the foe, to smother him. Not fully
Is earth smothered. Through certain dozens of flaws
In his hater's strength he has thinly, grimly forced
A stemless weed that, flat around every fissure,
Grips tight the gripper, as though the two were fused.

The asphalt looks like an old, enormous shell
Seized, this cranny and that, by green starfish.
They are small, but several. Cupped starfish strength
Sucks, sucks. It is presently checked by seasonal
Death. The shell will outwear any single
Counter-attacker. More will clutch it in spring.

Emblem: Beaver

Away across there, where dusk and the hovering woods
Darken the lake, something is swimming; I watch
A line's slow extension over the water
As I might watch, perhaps, the gradual wake
Of a silver pencil on dark grey paper. Were it
Feasible to fly with the homing heron and widen
My angle of sight, I should see two lines: a wedge,
Or, better, an arrow in slow flight, winging
Toward some target obscure in the blurred world.

What does it point at? A question more easily answered
In terms of time than of space. If the swimming animal,
The living, penetrating tip of the arrow,
Should be, improbably, a wolf or a broad-antlered
Moose, or a bear, I should know that the shaft was aimed
At the past: at wider and darker woods, adjoining
Broader, deeper, more sovereign lakes than any
You can find now. If the tip is only an active
Muskrat, the aim is the present: at fat, actual
Clams and lily roots, a burrow in mud authentically
Mud. But really, I think, the tip is an able
Beaver; the aim: the future — the not arrived.

All his sign-writing says that the mind of a beaver
Is never so much on the willow or alder bark
He eats today, as it is on trying to bring
A situation about that is really beyond
His beaver foresight, just to find out what bearing
It may have on him when it gets here. Viz, the big
Dam now crammed in the frustrated creek between
This lake and the next: did the labor gang benefit
From killing by drowning maybe a thousand birch

Saplings they never cut? No honeycomb black
With fussy bees, though, seems to be more of a boil
Of action than a rising dam with the beavers busy.

Offhand, it is odd how beavers seem increasing
Among us. You can find by cowering creeks
Where the feet of the suburbs are already clumping
Fresh white chips where the signature is chiseled.
It is as though our beavers and our country
Acknowledge a metaphorical consanguinity:
Swimmers in dark water, and great at cutting
Things down, in order to see what future will come.

Place Considered as a Time Factor

Close under bluff, in the insignificant talus
That wind, frost, or the prairie rains have tumbled
To the muddy edge of a prairie creek's trickle,
Plant your feet firmly; look up. You cannot traject
Your sight at right angles; hence you will see no trace
Of the fat new houses affronting the territory
A little back from the edge. There is only the twisting
Line of wild grass, wind-shaken, transected thrice
By wind-gnawed cedars and a broken burr oak torn
By wind. And the prairie sky, intense and timeless.

That is the setting; nothing about it has changed
Since the last morning a wandering bison came
To the edge to look down. Stare hard; confront him.
The big brown head, the massive oval, is calm
In knowledge that nothing in the world calls for caution
But a few weak arrows, and certain wolves and coyotes.
His beard hangs heavy; there is wind in his brown curls.

Of Cabbages and Kings

The peas that I planted too late in Kansas
Leaped to the light, into it, through it.
They were all extension; they never thickened
In stem enough, or darkened enough in leaf.
An inch a day at the least, and then blossoms
Not the plump popcorn of proper blossoms
But something like bits of the shabby wings
Of cabbage butterflies dead of butterfly age.
The pods hardly formed. Then the sun, good servant
Of peas in their time, became the bad master
Of peas that were late. The stalks went paler and limper.
Shortly, the mildew that lurks
For peas that are late, came sneaking up from the ground
Stem by stem, and quickly finished the job.
I, in some sense responsible
For making peas prove they are not salamanders,
Can do nothing in restitution but notice
That the ruined vines make excellent metaphors.

The World of the Hammerhead Shark

White, straw-colored, red: zinnias and hollyhocks.
Green mass and pale spots: apple tree with apples.
(And a dead bit on top, with leaves rotten-apple colored.)
Those are outside. On the table in front of me
The eggs and cutlery of breakfast. On the wall
A stuffed baby hammerhead shark, maybe two feet long.

I should riffle five years' worth of calendars
To find four dates I have been here.
An hour-hand would circle just twice
To count my time in this trivial joint by a highway.
I know it exactly, though, when I enter:
Here is another world I have made by seeing it.

I feel disquiet — perhaps of responsibility?
By this time of life, what a terrible clutter of worlds
I have certified in being, by using my senses!
I cannot unmake, neither at all improve them;
Only acknowledge, and possibly give them names.
The one this morning is the world of the hammerhead shark.

The Owl Ball

Not-wanting-to-do
Makes thighs heavy, slackens the calf muscles.
Feeling-there-is-no-
Point-in-it-all draws down the mouth's corners.
And then one would gladly make a Whitmanian turn
And live with animals, for their comforting unconcern
With evaluation, their direct doing what they do.

In the woods lately I came on an owl ball.
When I poked it apart, I saw it contained all
The usual items of owly regurgitation
(Feathers, and fur, and little white naked bones),
And something to boot: the hard legs and the feet
Of a crow, with the horny scales entire and complete,
And the claws complete, in their perfect scratchy blackness.

The tough barred owl, as he made his meal in the night,
Was troubled, I judge, by no hesitation at all.
Nevertheless, it is somewhat puzzling to know
What to think of that startlingly thorough eating of crow.

In a strip of old prairie, paradoxically spared
For lying close beside a destructive agent
Of prairies, a railway, I remember one could in season
Go hunting lilies. Of course not the over-scented,
Under-colored domestic lilies that speak
From funeral houses and altars of death and resurrection.
Rather, wild tiger lilies, low-scented, high-colored,
With petals recurved like snarls, black-spotted on orange.
One time I saw them leaning over the bones
Of (possibly) a prairie chicken caught on her nest by fire.
They seemed a right tribute to honor a wild death.
As for resurrection — they nodded in the prairie wind.

Loon-Link

Loon cry, under the late, round moon
So pure silver, as from a silver trumpet:
Of all the means of linkage, the many, many
Connectives, what a good one, how thrilling,
To fly, to tie together the spread mazes
Of lakes, each bound in its own night thickets;

Long, smooth, silver, trumpeting cry
Rising perhaps from the cattail bay on Henry
To fly on every compass arrow; to carry
To cold and empty Lost, to Pleasant that has
Shores thick in pine; to flicker up choked creeks
To Sunset, to Dewdrop, on to the potholes ahead;

To glance over Big Star, green, and Little Star, blue
(Silver, arrowing call from the throat of a loon),
And black-looking Beaver, its shore with a down birch
Where sometimes a wood duck perches; to touch shut lilies
Locked in their pads on Round; at last to bring
To someone awake, a richness of night lakes.

II

If I had existed without benefit
Of (God stop the mouthful!) the Industrial Revolution,
Probably I should have been a doubly poor farmer,
Caught between memories of grim childhood
And anticipations of grisly age;
Caught between the snow, the mud, and the dust;
Toothless at forty, and ruptured, and widowed;
Not giving a damn for the winds of Heaven.

These images do not reconcile me with Heaven
For sprawling me into a time widowed
Of quiet forever, it seems (though the dust
Of H-bomb testing suggests for the age
Its burial service); when even childhood
Is one blank stereotype; when the farmer
Is bookkeeper-mechanic; and constant revolution
Of wheels is considered man's greatest benefit.

Unto the Second Generation

When his father walked in the woods, the pines
Bowed flat to him; he made their long trunks float
Pike-darted stream to mill, to be his wealth.
Quacking mallards of fall to his hidden boat
Plunged for his proper dinner; and the mink
And beaver shed their richest coats for him
To question whose control was vain as if
The pines should have implored he pity them.

Wild things grow independent; the pines draw
Far back from stump-filled farms; the pike and trout
Bite for the summer anglers; mallards veer
In thin lines far from blind; in summer drought
Mud shows few tracks of fur-rich courtiers.
All these deny him wealth, or well-clothed limb,
To try to make whom lord is vain as if
He should implore the pines they pity him.

Though the rough, bitter-sweet haw of pioneering
Seems now as remote as wheat in Egyptian tomb,
Grandparents actually ate it. In the big weather,
Under a strange heaven's gigantic bloom,
Between huge lakes, on huge prairies they dwelled.

And testified later: though dying children could tell you
That frontier doctors were dangerous as disease;
Though hail, tornado, or the cow in the kitchen garden
Could so disappoint as to make the heart freeze,
Those were their finest years, the first on the prairie.

Yes. The blue-grey devils of nature are only wild,
And stubborn; and seldom dangerous in the end.
To valiant aggressors they give the flushing gift
Of victory softly, almost as to a friend.
It is hidden that they were the easy enemy,

Until those other devils, that should be red
From long enough pickling in the juice of the human heart,
By pressure and raid make conquerors realize
That an older, harder war is still at its start.
They long for the easy diversion, but that is gone.

A New Inhabitant of Heaven

He rises early in a summer morning
And strolls to see the perfectly blooming flowers
That shine all softly down the long garden
Still dewy tender in those early hours.

Nothing distracts him save a mild envy
Of the gardeners who garden the whole day,
Or perhaps of the head groom out in the spacious stables
Petting the handsome black and lovely bay.

He need choose only whether day and evening
Shall pass between the high, book-lichened walls
Of his own library, through whose wide windows
Come sheep-bell tunes, and gentle bird calls;

Or whether, to the door of his English castle
Shall come admiring friends of his own choice
To sit beside him on the shaded terrace
And listen with pleasure to his friendly voice.

The Spring Potomac

Force of the season flashes the bird north
And the fish shearing up cold currents to spawn.
At this time fishermen stand on the banks of rivers.
Along the Potomac they huddle on every rock
From before light comes till after the light is gone.

A seasonal rite performed in happiness:
Fish blood stiffened on fingers, perhaps, allows
Timbre of friendliness in voices that call
From rock to rock, and voices that fondly curse
The act of their pleasure, there where the water flows.

Rain in Virginia curtains the gentle redbud.
In the youngest leaves, what cool and delicate green.
After the ritual, fishermen drive back home
Sweeter in soul, they think, athletic in mind,
Their tempers purged of the winter's sooty spleen.

Yet I have a vision, here on my fishing rock
Beside the medicinal river. Like an old wall
The river reaches. It carries the ghostly print
Of a million unwitting prayers and lamentations
Flung by men nostalgia-gnawn at soul.

And the casting hands of the fishermen silently strike it.
In silence the ghostly cry of an old regret:
"May our strength fail, oh, may our right hands wither
If we forget thee, time of our simple fathers,
And our breath dry in our throats, if we forget!"

When the World Was Young

Its value? I can make no assessment.
But I like to unroll, sometimes,
This image, enscrolled safely
Within skull, central in the section
Of pictures of hope and sunniness.

From the new door of a new house, a woman
Comes with her blanketed baby, and sprightly walks
Under that well-wishing sun that the sky wears
In northern early summer. How can her work,
A half-pioneer farm wife's daily wrestle,
Be left? Perhaps can't. Nevertheless, watch;
She is going. There birds. Flowers. Everywhere, wealth
Of the best unbroken green of a young world.

And now she stops, spreads in that freshness
The blanket, lays on it the baby to lie fisting
The air, and patiently out of the foliage
Close round about, gathers the gem-red fruiting
Of wild strawberries. Soon she has finished
(So rich is that richness), and walks homeward, fetching
On one arm the baby, in one hand a basketed feasting
Of the small red berries, of all fruit I know most fragrant.

Today the stream of consciousness must follow
An asphalt bed, shallow in the endless world
Of untried dust and still gold flowers in Kansas,
Peaks not controlled, faith-grasped like religion,
And sage-gaunt plain, extension's bare region.

My poor brain, whirled leaf-like down the surface,
Groping to fix this present by some past,
Grows wry with exegetic fantasies.
"What price movement to the known?" keeps crying
That knowledge come to man in one place lying.

A colored film, oblivion's destined booty,
Unrolls, traveler's lone reward, and frail.
The flowers shine on the sky as drawn on paper.
In two dimensions lopes the scuffed coyote.
No rooms are back of house fronts seen in city.

The Nature of Jungles

Every day, walking the city streets,
He conned within himself the nature of jungles,
Enlarged his mind for poisonous thorns and flies,
And green mambas secret in green tangles.

Under his eyes, vultures degraded death,
And noosing lianas flourished by strangulation;
The worms and shrews under the endless muck
Ate each other in endless repetition.

Every day he perused the paradox,
What grisly fashion life with life mingles;
And saw the teeth that shone for his jugular
Every day, walking the city jungles.

Crusted with soil, and the soil forest-matted;
Brooded by peaks, and the peaks in lawless cloud,
The enemy: that black, amorphous ore,
That earth-demon, waiting to be combatted.

So the plans came, precise as circle or square,
And the shapely tools, like tamed, treacherous beasts.
You have heard the ode that lauds that short fight;
You know the discipline forced on the conquered there.

Some of it, then, was moulded to smooth cars
To hurry with ease on the smooth, exact roads;
Some, that is, must implement man's dream
Of docile speed, sifted of checks and jars —

Till the shattering crash, and the dreamed-up shape gone,
The metal turned scrap, and the scrap readied for rust;
Someone, too, crushed to chaos of man,
The pattern crushed that his members were strung upon.

For the Enemy was not ore, under disarranged
Mountains conquered, or yoked when the trees fell.
Under the plan, in the conqueror's own breast,
Forever pumps the Enemy heart, unchanged.

The Meaning of a Scene

One walking in that morning-by-the-clock
Went humbled as a man with skin and club
Through a pre-fire convention of dark and cold.
Metallic ground, rime on the willows and old
Grass. Even the first light, crowded thin
By the planet's shadow, was only like the light
Of the moon in an Arctic steely with its snow.

The odds were hopeless for the burning wick
That flickered, single in shack rearing alone,
Against the quality that lay outside.
How should it, puniness that must abide
Shadows in corners, iciness on floor,
Conquer the essence of the space between the stars?

It did not. The universe being no kind of game,
And even no war, the dark-cold and the lamp
Were stedfast in their non-relationship.
The first contracted living in its grip
Until, light pushing wide, the red sun rolled
The horizon at last, and brought the warming day.
The second helped some bachelor farmer pay
His duty to washing, dressing, and suchlike
Until his visible breath had puffed it out,
And he shivered barnward tracking the pale frost.

Virginia mountains, though small for mountains, rise
Beyond the range of houses. In early winter,
With a first little snow to pick out the brown trees
And scent the clear air spilling so far down
To the valley, one is gratified by these.
From the artificiality of the car,
One says, How fine natural things are.
One says, Yes, the peace of natural mountains.

In the ridge's shadow, where yesterday's thaw spilled
Snow water, there is ice on the road this morning.
A car must follow its artificial track;
It hits the ice. Then the force of brute momentum
Delivers its irresistible attack
Upon the driver's convenient artifice.
One gasps, Lord, not so natural as this!
One gasps, I am not made for a meteorite!

Skidding feels like a kind of political lesson:
One emerges impressed anew with the need of checks
And balances. This does not mean to stay
Home when the winter air lies on the uplands
More than when they allow the colors of May.
One thinks, The artificial will only permit
Brief look at natural mountains as they sit
Under such conditions that I can relish it.
One thinks, The unchecked naturalness of death!

Suburban Flower Store, Washington, D.C.

It is, yes, December still, the old year.
A few bowl football games are still to play;
These justify, if you like, the yellow display
Of chrysanthemums on half the counter here.
Anyhow, the chrysanthemums suggest the old year.

But tomorrow is January, start of the new,
And in January in even the upper South
The first warm sighs murmur from spring's mouth.
It isn't unreasonable to have on view
All these jonquils, spring and yellow and new.

Yet, Lord, the autumn I think is evil days:
"Food and life!" cry the pleasant fruits that fall;
But they hurry, hurry to mildewy death, and all
The hungry cold of winter's negative ways.
There is too much contradiction in those days.

And Spring as bad, for the world at last resigned
To the long, flat, drugging quiet of death
Is stabbed alive with the pain of first breath
Only to see the flowers, how they go on the wind;
And to that, of course, we have never been resigned.

So I think it rawly unfair there be set together
These signal flowers from the days that trouble me most.
A man is entitled to his stretch of killing frost
Between the excitements of spring and of fall weather,
And not both meteorological griefs together!

Picture Framed by a Streetcar Window

What was it daubed on their shoulders by that old light?
(For this is the point: the color of fire is old.)
I saw, expressed from the morning shadowy cold,
Some muffled fellows bending to warm their hands
At a fire; but the feel of the picture was not right.

The fire lit all the essential stoop and blur
Of the basic emergent biped. Their background was
The building they had not finished, and that rose
A Euclidean huge abstraction into the dawn
As though it would box even the morning star.

There was the check. A thing to impose its lines
On the very dome of the lordly ellipsing seven
Could square to its squareness, surely, any given
Mammalian morsel — what could the builders do
But submit to the structure's angular confines?

Yet the old fire figured a manness into the men
Older than structures, which said they would shortly walk
Simply away; go shelter beside old rock
Or under old forest, but never by wrung steel
Till it reddened and wept into oldest earth again.

A Fifty-Year-Old Smiling Public Man

Conceive now, a man devoured by a pack of wolves,
A huge pack, of such assiduous appetite
No morsel of heart or brain escaped the gorging.
Conceive next, a weirdly inverted apotheosis,
And here is our man again, with a broader smile,
But wolf, pure wolf, to the last heart's atom.
Any stray lambs had better view with alarm.

I remember how it went, though, before they fanged him down;
The scene was Hollywood out of pre-Soviet Russia.
There were stars, and a whistling sleigh, and pounding horses,
And he turned with a rifle to fire at the red rapine
Of the nearest throats, and the sickening horses floundered,
And the dark mass gained, rather flowing than running,
And the gap was closed, and he snapped off his last round.

Aleut or pre-Aleut is dead.
See (if the fogs of Umnak will allow)
How someone, liaison with the verities,
Stoops in the white and wet above him; how

He guts him through the pelvis or the chest.
He oils him rightly, binds him chin to knee
In a netted pack of seal or sea-lion skin,
And launches with him on the idiot sea

To some swirled islet, empty and difficult.
There, in a steamy cave, he adds him to
A stack along the wall; or else, outside,
Digs in the ocean soil that never grew

A plant but moss, a minimal square grave.
Lacking sarcophagus, he uses wrack
From storms on woodier shores to line this place
Of mystery; and then he hurries back

Through the wind's danger, where the living are.
The next day, probably, he catches seals.
His work is done as media permit,
But doubtless that is adequate, one feels,

To let the Aleut soul declare — although
It sit eternity in that wan place
Not greatly denser than the sea and fog,
And sit there, maybe, with its mummy's face

Ruined by puffins or the irreverent fox —
That life is truly, as a man would wish,
Some unit more than can be measured by
Its total bag of sea lions, gulls, and fish.

III

Sitting in the Woods: A Contemplation

I

Here am I, a shape under a cedar,
And all the world takes bearings on the shape.
An oak-sitting squirrel, wary for quick escape,

Yet pins me with his eye. A jittery wren,
Though he clings to his skinny twig upside down,
Pins me. Under my back and legs, the brown

Cedar needles record exactly a weight;
Over my face and belly and hands, the warm,
Cedary air records exactly a form.

Every leaf on certain thousands of twigs,
Each stone nearby, and berry and haw and hip
Notes that there is exact relationship

Of degree, minute, and second, on a certain plane,
Between itself and the shape I thought was free,
Sprawled in the woods under a cedar tree.

II

That giant Gulliver was not so bound
By all those cables the little men drew tight
As I by this amazing cobweb of right

Records and measurements. Now, can one center
A web like this, with the number of strands so great,
And then, by his single will and his single weight,

Break loose? Will it not be a complaisant ghost
That smiles tonight in the room where I should appear,
While I stay under the cedar, fixed here?

Rustle-rustled the breeze straight from the moon,
And the moon struck yellow in the hunter's lifting eyes.
Were sabre-tooth tigers yellow? No hides persist,
But Bengal tigers are in half their stripes,

And lions are yellow, and leopards and jaguars are,
And jackals snarling in African village fight.
And the round spot circling and curving over the grass
From a flashlight to bolster the glow of the moon tonight.

Yellowish strips that snap like rubber bands
Are night-crawlers seized when the neighbors lie in bed
By the hunter's hands tanned yellow, meant to lure
Small trout to spill their poor veins' innocent red.

Angina Pectoris

The steady heart, which in its steadiness
Allows formation of the somewhat, life,
Unsteadies, stops, and so a thick debris
Drops to the sidewalk, where the poor limbs sprawl
Like things a child had made of mud, and all
The color leaves the face, pale as a knife.

When the man walked down the street in his mackinaw,
Or sat in a barroom gurgling at his beer,
It was only a small usurper of oxygen
I noticed; I'd have seen him ship for Spain,
Or go to Dakota and die working with grain,
And never thought, or been glad he was not here.

But now that I see him neutral earth, to bury
In earth, for damp, or a pale, poetic swarm
Of worms to end, I'm sorry; I wish him what
I'd not wish other mud: that he ate tonight
With children he loved, that the meal was heavy and right,
That he slept with plenty of quilts to keep him warm.

Sentimental Reflection

Crumpled, disappointing substitute
For any kind of letter from anyone at all,
Here's nothing in the mailbox except an *Alumni
Monthly,* coming unwanted as usual,
Like some poor dog that will get no praise for pursuit.

Tear the thin brown wrapper, and inspect
Without approval, the picture of college stone
Or college faces; then from the slippery sheets
Begin to read the names of people you've known;
Do it in idleness, nothing at all to expect.

Begin, though, to see that old scene
Of foothill and fir tree, marvelous fall air.
View implies a viewer, you realize
— And here's yourself, as you used to walk there,
Yourself minus fifteen years, what you have been.

Flowers may not turn with suns, but men turn
Sometimes to look at years; the difference
Between *then* and *now* is the cant of your face
Toward that intervening sequence
Of time, that chunk checking your own return.

If value's much defined by scarcity,
Oneself, in the fix of this or that old year,
Is valuable, and not in Narcissus' terms,
When really got back, and seen clear:
Carbon's a jewel, when its type's a rarity.

Brown wrapper, composition of a butcher's sack,
Contains real meat and blood, and they are your own.
A letter, to give you portion of someone else,
Is a happier take, but this is a rarer one,
Letter to yourself, from the hard-known back track.

Old Theme

Perhaps disrespectful to Villon to put it so, but
Where are the cells of yesteryear?
Where are the teeth the bones the blood the gullet
Comfortably yours just seven years ago?
It isn't a light inquiry. One does not care
Into what sewer the snow ran, or into what bog;
But it isn't that way about the firmer flesh
And the twenty-twenty vision of twenty-two.

I remember, as a boy, by the water,
How the fish, in the evening, flashed silver
As they sloshed on the surface, playing or eating flies.
I do not think now of the grey-blue grace of the water,
Admire the aesthetic in fish, or else the athletic.
I recall instead that the scaly flashing resembled
Silver, durable metal.

It had not tarnished when, a long time later,
Evening dimmed over me and the same water.
I reflected that fish have even more tragedies
Than the nightingale Keats told lies about; each
Generation has always its sons spiked in its jaws.
But my teeth my bones my blood my gullet
Cried out that the rising, flashing fish resembled
Silver, durable metal.

After Leaf-Fall

Bare branches of late autumn reach in patience
Toward the torn and raining autumn sky.
They hold my torn heart in their waving crotches.

Old people, with a fair amount of grace,
Move quietly toward the time they die.
They manipulate their recollections well.

Young people, scuffling by in rainy pairs,
Have reasonable luck in what they try.
They scuffle home to the light and radio.

Houses, taking the weather on their walls,
Have merit for the shelter they supply.
They sit dirty and dim, but they sit solid.

All black and bare, the autumn limbs extend
Toward the autumn clouds where no birds fly.
They hold my heart extended unto Heaven.

Old Clothes

Limply the gatherings of guns ride home
In shooting-coat pockets; relic feathers and hairs
In mine are trivial monuments to lairs
Empty somewhere along my back track.
And still I go at it: climbing on wind-worn hills
Scheming for gun-sight on Kansas cottontails.

Pheasant that, shot-struck, held in the hollow air
A moment, and fell, even then was a kind of dream.
Now, layered under by years, what thing can he seem
But a kind of ghost of the onetime dream of a sight?
Still doggedly lugging a gun for the cottontails,
What is it, I wonder, I have shot out of other hills?

Ghosts may gibber for themselves; the thing I could never
Smooth into pocket is any pattern or part
Of a world or a time where this idiocy of the heart
Could goad me to gunning but never to making reasons:
Where, for an hour, I could clamber the windy hills
Without asking definitions of cottontails.

Once, in this region, were a straggle of reddish men
Whose basic definition of life was the buffalo.
When they knew that the beasts were going, must wholly go,
They panted in magic dances to bring them back.
Sometimes I think that I pant on the prairie hills
In a ghost dance, really, after more than cottontails.

Position: Oregon Trail

Except beneath the blur of a winter sky,
Where in the name of measurement am I
(We know ourselves, we live, by measurement)
This edgeless day? Oh, a knoll and a swale
North of the Oregon Trail.

Let me go south, then, a swale and a knoll
Over wearily tawny grass, where bushes thole
In the indeterminate purple of the season,
And make a considering stop. But my eyes fail
To find the Oregon Trail.

Paveless trace, it is merged with the ground and gone.
A dozen such could fade in the life of a man.
(That mark no wheel rut — only the run of rabbits.)
My cast for placement is spoiled; the years prevail
Over the Oregon Trail.

But not, possibly, over the softling hills
Nuzzling into the greyness the sky spills
(They do look worn; to flint-men they looked the same)
There yonder? With no such sneer shall time assail
Them as the Oregon Trail.

Wait. The lightest wind that can bend a shoot
Is weapon enough; the scrape of a coyote's foot.
There needs no catastrophe that breaks all measure.
They shall be sent by the drag of a mouse's tail
To join the Oregon Trail.

All hesitancy of color and line today
Is a view of time carrying place away.
(How do I look, I wonder, in my own blotched khaki?)
In the sprawl of winter, there's no help hearing a tale
About the Oregon Trail.

Big Dam

Muddy meek river, oh, it was splendid sport
Those times you tore apart tranquility
And swam the gar through frightened village streets
(And sent the villagers to live in tents)
And spread your silted bed on every sort
Of floor, and rammed the prairie at the sea —
But where, do you think, is the end of suchlike feats?
Good Lord, did you never hear of consequence?

Look, do you see your wedge of tumult spread?
Words rage like water, and all Congress frowns,
And tit for tat, and the world witnesses
You shall be damned and dammed for tumult's sake —
And swim the carp above the milking shed
(And send the farmers off to live in towns)
And try if cedars can be cypresses
And lose the arid prairie in a lake.

— As for me, I limit my claim hereabout
To a handful of berries (wild) from the thorny bank;
Yet the heart turns a little at seeing wreckage.
Though algae thicken in calm on shallowing stones
And an innocent babyhood of willows sprout
Fishbone-thick on the bar's widening flank —
See, in the under bend, a huge flung breakage
Of bone-white cottonwood boles, white as old bones.

Grackle Days

A badge of this weather is the yellow leaf
Falling — not fallen, not of the compost heap
Dead, yet, but slanting the nearer sky
In a last illusion before the long, quiet
Period of change follows.
                        Another badge
Is the shining wings, the nervous wings, that add
More twinkling units to the high trees, I think,
Than the planing leaves subtract, though the color they bring
Is black, with purple and blue.
                        The slim grackles
Tweak, creak, squeak; how they clitter and clatter!
The wrinkling rush in a riffle of turning minnows
Suggests what the movement in trees full of grackles is.

For a boy ornithologist, grackles should be convenient
Subjects: not rare or abstruse. I have not seen
Better detail than grackles for a kind of *genre*
Landscape painting, if an artist cared to arm
His patience to use them. How about color film
For a nature photographer, and a vibrant limb
Of October grackles? Also, they say, the black
Creakers make pie that is fairly palatable.

I need fall's grackles, of course, for flatly nothing
I can list with my cataloguing head: the stuff
Of recognition is heartstuff, and lives below
Brow level, and gathers none of its vital knowing
From page or canvas or any museum usage.
But let the turning feathers release the fused
Purple and blue particular iridescence
In the air of these grackle days; heartleap comes then.

Prairie August

I

A good image (although it must come about
Through the mind's involuntary mosaic-making
From heat spots scrambling before my affronted eyes):
Low, long butte, and the grass plain rolling out
Of vision entirely; quietly there, not breaking
Pattern at all, the slender shelters of nomads.

I see no people, but see that their dwellings grow
Native in the land as a thicket of thorny plum.
The owners wander wide in the clashing wind
And the wind is brother. Their clots of horned wealth flow
Through pastures no metal touches. The sun-spears from
Heaven hurt them no more than they hurt lizards.

II

Retire now, image. Not your affair to oppose
What I commonly see, and call real. I think the weather
Honors no passports, in aliens sees no friends.
Crash! comes the sun on my angular house it knows
Should have stayed in New England. Fiercely the winds gather
Fierce, metal-raised dust from the harried miles

To sift on my moveless floor. And shall I arise,
Go dampen my soul in the artificial lake?
I never see it, such oddly limp-looking water,
Without thinking that even the water sighs
For distant edges where elegant birch leaves shake
Approval over the digging of old glaciers.

One genius of the place, though, grins in the weather's eye;
I will go and admire him. Where an athletic current
Flows warm as milk calf-drawn from a bison's teat
(And brown as a bison) on limestone breakings that lie
As they were spread by the last flood's torrent:
There, the channel cat. There, lively, he whisks

From riffle to riffle; there, in the muddy rush
His humorous whiskers spread; and the palpitation
Of his arching gills, and the turn of his graceful flank
Acknowledge satisfied kinship with all they touch.
"Ha, ha!" he cries from his current to all creation.
He seems to laugh even on a fish stringer.

Little-League Baseball Fan

No closer the glove clings to the sweaty hand
Than clings my drybones heart
To the being of greenbones there where he jumps and hollers
For the batter to get a hit;
Then comes himself to the proof, the plate, holding
The long bat heavy
And strong to reverse the flight of the whirling, humming
Pitch: sock it like hell.

Lord knows what kind of mystery puts together
Into one flesh the two
Of drybones and greenbones. Yet his every twitch,
Every glint of triumph
At having mastered the ball's trajectory
Is mine, mine too.
I am warm, thoughtless, grinning into the twilight;
My flesh glows, and I thrill.

So be it. For maybe a glow of flesh will cancel
A cold vision clutched
Under the flesh, in my long bones' cells:
Everyman-Me confronting
(Unwilling batter) in a game that will not continue
Many more outs, the crossfire
Of the daily sun. And my God, who could connect
With those impossible curves?

A wandering dream tells me that it is shameful
To have grown so old, to have come to this very spring,
In any employment that takes less tax of my senses
And more of my impecunious nerves, than, say,
Working by a lakeside, caulking the spread seams
Of some old boat, while above me the hillside snow
Grows mushy at last in the equinoctial sun,
And watery margins invite the first ducks from the South.

Of the Difficulty of Map-Reading

Heraclitus: the best soul is the driest soul
But the soul delights to get wet. Very well, my sinner:
I think a map of *your* soul would be black with spots
Denoting bogholes, where ooze bubbles and sucks;
And arsenical green with spots denoting sloughs
Where algae sicken, and rotting lily pads stink;
And sulphurous yellow with spots that stand for stretches
Where damp fungi flourish, mostly the species
That, beaten by rain, deliquesce most soddenly,
Or breathe the worst malodor when the foot stirs them,
Or attract most insects, and those most ugly and slimy.

Curse you. But I wonder: if all those dampest
Pictures are symbols, to signify your damnation,
Are the further pictures that the inner eye discovers
Symbols as well, to complicate all decision?
Note well: where the lips of bogholes are blackest dirty,
The blooms of the jewelweed may glow their deepest;
Recall: where the trash of sloughs is the saddest dull,
The brood of the shy grebe may dip most daintily;
Let the eye remember: what surprisingly delicate
Hues of pastel shimmer from many different
Mushrooms, even if they grow where woods are darkest.

When I cut my thumb in Nebraska City,
I left some blood in the local clay.
When, in Knoxville, that baseball clipped me,
I spat a tooth by a Tennessee creek.
The time I pared my nails in Cheyenne,
The little moons blew in Wyoming wind.

Do I enrich some tall, winy
Hollyhock in Nebraska weather?
Exist as a cyst in the ugly, wrinkled
Gut of a turtle in Tennessee water?
Maybe I toughen the toughly wearing
Stem of a stick of Wyoming sage.

From what bald eagle did I get, let's say,
The little black mole above my stomach?
Am I the debtor of a leopard shark
For the calloused places that thicken my soles?
Possibly the atoms of a vanished spruce
Are linked in the whorls of my mammal's brain.

The records of debt and credit belly
In the winds of the interstellar blanks,
Or somewhere as reachless. That columns balance,
If anybody's, is God's business.
For me, it is duty enough to bestow
Interest on this existing pattern

That sits in my chair holding my pencil.
Any indebtedness, present or possible,
To shark, or eagle, or tree of the prime,
Will have to be canceled (who would protest it?)
By the easy and casual presentation
Of the pattern constructing now: this poem.

I

In boylight, near Wausau, Wisconsin,
A long time ago, a summer foray or picnic
Into the glimmer of light on deep water
And the glitter on shallow water
And the shine on leaves and on berries
(Going to Lake Wausau, we called it):
Golden, golden weather; golden age.
Presently, berrying or bullheading finished,
And evening fragility beginning to show in colors,
A start toward home.

II

A big-boled pine stood close to the river once.
When the loggers had finished their job,
The stump they left had a top blandly smooth
And blandly horizontal. Later, a small dam
Sent water exploring. It found the meaty stump
And claimed and covered it; not very deep, just enough
For assimilation. And sometime, someone
Built a boat (possibly, out of the pine's lumber);
A boyboat, really, with bottom blandly smooth
And blandly horizontal.

III

O, lovely the fading gladiolus hues on water
Darkened to herald night. Pleasantly strange
The staggering Z's of the first flying of bats.
Romantic the zoom of the swoop of cruising nighthawk.

Why try to look out for a stump
Under the surface, when one is hurrying home?
The oar stroke that grated us home on the covered top
No other stroke could undo. The boat hung still
As the sky above it. In trees on shore
The squawk of the latest blue jay elided into
The first owl-trill.

IV

Proposition: Although one wants to get home,
Does he have, if the way there leads up-current,
To move to arrive? For will not his home
Come, inevitably, creeping down-current
To him? Not just waterside stuff picked up
By a rise; and familiar tannery taint
(Though those will come). Will not the interest
Of those who saw him go off down-current as though
Down-time, be distilled from hearts and from brooding eyes
Brooding on the river; will it not enter the water,
And come, and reach him? And if this isn't the same
As going, and reaching a home that waited unmoved,
Will he know the difference?

V

The struggle in darkness, shoving, shifting;
The empty heaving at a useless fulcrum —
I remember these. Growing silent
And listening, so, to the smallest sounds of darkness,
The plops and gurgles near, and the tiny
Rustling and calling yonder in the dark shoreward —

I remember that. What I do not remember
Is ever feeling pine wood moving on pine wood
Until we were off. Can I say that we did get off?
Or do we sit in a boat on a carrying river
That bears and brings us the life we live
In boynight, near Wausau, Wisconsin?

Fire and Fire

Summer prunings of bushes piled
On a bare round of soil burned empty
With consumption of such as summer prunings:
A tangle of slender stems half dead,
But through them, and fairly thick on top,
A lacing of leaves that need not have died yet.

I strike a match. The drier twigs
Accept, tentatively, the flame.
It spreads through the leafless lower tangle
Of the pile, a yellow background now
For the very temporary green
Of the thin, delicate, foreground leaves.

The rising gases that start to curl them
Bring smoky heat to my tilted face,
And trigger a fancy or recollection:
For a moment, I seem to lose judgment
Of the fire's dimensions; I seem to look at
Thick, long flames that whisk to ashes

Not twigs, but the trunks of forest trees;
And may burn me, except for the shielding
Those fragile, dying leaves can give.
Then I notice heat from above.
The shielding tree-head that is above
Has gaps and crevices; through them shows

The yellow sky-fire of the sun
Like a forest fire pressing the branches:
Fire tall as the steep sky,
To fall with the brooding sky's weight

On the whole world of the vegetable
And the whole world of the animal

If anything there escapes the death
My little flaring match released.
How precious, how precarious
My shields below, above! Dismayed,
I shrink between the green and green
That shrink between the fire and fire.

Night Wind in Fall

Air heaves at matter:
The wind makes all the wind noises.
Twig-strain, leaf-scatter,
Tapping of tips on rebuffing windows,
Nut-fall, little shatter
Of rotted small limbs on blunting ground.
Neither metronomic nor constant,
But recurring as metres recur.

I remember "Words alone
Are certain good." I don't hear,
Either in twig-tap, blown-
Leaf sigh, or hissing or whistle
Or scrape, the singular tone
Of a word. Inarticulate wind.
Yet a rising and falling persists.
Words are a rising and falling.

Someone less drowsy
Than I am, might understand,
Might catch, from mousy
Sounds and silences, birdlike
Alternations, from ghostly
Stutters, a viable pattern of words.
Unclogged senses might do it.
There must be senses unclogged

Somewhere. Maybe, I think,
They can decode such words
As bless, from brink to brink,
The whole reach that listens under the wind.

I hope each chink, each link
That forms this house is blessed. And all
Houses. All of the running grass.
Every lake in Canada under the stars.

Distinguished books of contemporary poetry
available in cloth-bound and paperback editions
published by Wesleyan University Press

Alan Ansen:	*Disorderly Houses* (1961)
John Ashbery:	*The Tennis Court Oath* (1962)
Robert Bagg:	*Madonna of the Cello* (1961)
Robert Bly:	*Silence in the Snowy Fields* (1962)
Tram Combs:	*St. Thomas. poems.* (1965)
Donald Davie:	*New and Selected Poems* (1961)
James Dickey:	*Drowning With Others* (1962)
James Dickey:	*Helmets* (1964)
David Ferry:	*On the Way to the Island* (1960)
Robert Francis:	*The Orb Weaver* (1960)
Richard Howard:	*Quantities* (1962)
Barbara Howes:	*Light and Dark* (1959)
David Ignatow:	*Figures of the Human* (1964)
David Ignatow:	*Say Pardon* (1961)
Donald Justice:	*The Summer Anniversaries* (1960) (A Lamont Poetry Selection)
Chester Kallman:	*Absent and Present* (1963)
Vassar Miller:	*My Bones Being Wiser* (1963)
Vassar Miller:	*Wage War on Silence* (1960)
W. R. Moses:	*Identities* (1965)
Donald Petersen:	*The Spectral Boy* (1964)
Hyam Plutzik:	*Apples from Shinar* (1959)
Vern Rutsala:	*The Window* (1964)
Louis Simpson:	*At the End of the Open Road* (1963) (Pulitzer Prize in Poetry, 1964)
Louis Simpson:	*A Dream of Governors* (1959)
James Wright:	*The Branch Will Not Break* (1963)
James Wright:	*Saint Judas* (1959)